Dinner at a Queen's Table

Experiencing the World of Whole Foods for Beginners

Etta R. Collins

TEACH Services, Inc.
PUBLISHING
www.TEACHServices.com • (800) 367-1844

World rights reserved. This book or any portion thereof may not be copied or reproduced in any form or manner whatever, except as provided by law, without the written permission of the publisher, except by a reviewer who may quote brief passages in a review.

The author assumes full responsibility for the accuracy of all facts and quotations as cited in this book. The opinions expressed in this book are the author's personal views and interpretations, and do not necessarily reflect those of the publisher.

This book is provided with the understanding that the publisher is not engaged in giving spiritual, legal, medical, or other professional advice. If authoritative advice is needed, the reader should seek the counsel of a competent professional.

Copyright © 2022 Etta R. Collins

Copyright © 2022 TEACH Services, Inc.

ISBN-13: 978-1-4796-0908-6 (Paperback)
ISBN-13: 978-1-4796-0916-1 (ePub)
Library of Congress Control Number: 2021921076

The website references in this book have been shortened using a URL shortener and redirect service called 1ref.us, which TEACH Services manages. If you find that a reference no longer works, please contact us and let us know which one is not working so that we can correct it. Any personal website addresses that the author included are managed by the author. TEACH Services is not responsible for the accuracy or permanency of any links.

Acknowledgments

Special thanks to my son, Pastor Gary, who encouraged me to share my recipes in a cookbook. He also arranged the first draft of the manuscript. To my husband, Ed, who has supported me in every possible way. To my daughter, Arlette, who inspired me to move forward. Many thanks to my daughter-in-law, Loretta, who helped get this project off the ground, and to the many that coached me by persistently asking, "When is the cookbook coming out?" I'm grateful to all.

Table of Contents

Acknowledgments iii
Introduction... 7
Entrees 11
Baked Macaroni and Cheese 12
Baked Tofu.. 13
Barbecue Tofu 13
Cabbage Rolls 14
Choplets® Loaf 15
Delectable Vegetable Stew........................... 16
Haystacks Combo 17
Lasagna 18
Low-cal Chili 19
Pecan Meatballs..................................... 20
Pinto Beans and Brown Rice 21
Rolled Oat Patties................................... 22
Sausage and Noodle Casserole 23
Spaghetti and Pecan Meatballs 24
Tofu Cheese and Potato Supreme 25
Vege-links and Baked Beans 26
Vegeburger Loaf 27
Wok Vegetable Stir-fry with Tofu..................... 28
Vegetables... 29
Baby Lima Beans and Peas........................... 30
Banana and Sweet Potato Soufflé 31
Black-eyed Peas and Okra 32
Crunchy Cabbage and Red Bell Pepper 33
Fried Corn 33
Garlic Spinach 34
Honey Beets.. 35
Mixed Greens 36
Pan-Browned Potatoes 37
Peas with Sliced Almonds........................... 38
Savory Cauliflower and Zucchini..................... 38
Twice Baked Sweet Potatoes 39
Vegetable Platter................................... 40
Salads... 41
Best Tossed Salad 42
Carrot and Apple Salad 43
Macaroni Salad 44
Mixed Fruit Salad 45
Potato Salad....................................... 46
Taco Salad 46
Tomato and Cucumber Salad......................... 47
Vegetable and Spaghetti Salad....................... 48
Salad Dressings.................................... 49
Celery Dressing 50
Cucumber Dressing................................. 50
Honey Sesame Dressing............................. 51
Lip-smacking French Dressing 51
Marinade for Vegetable Platter...................... 52

Vegetable and Spaghetti Salad Dressing. 53

Sauces, Gravies, and Broth **55**
Ginger Sauce 56
Mom's Brown Gravy. 57
Nutty Yellow Cheese Sauce 58
Pizza Sauce. 59
Rolled Oat Patty Broth. 60

Side Dishes **61**
Baked French Fries. 62
Broccoli Rice 63
Cool Banana and Cherry Drink. 63
Easy Vegetable Soup. 64
Excellent Sandwich Spread 65
Flaky Brown Rice 66
Fruit Drink. 67
Fruit Pizza 68
Hearty Trail Mix 69
Make It Your Way Pizza 70
Scrambled Tofu 71
Spanish Rice 72

Desserts **73**
Banana Ice Cream. 74
Blueberry Crisp. 75
Coconut Macaroons 76
Easy Banana Pudding. 77
Famous Sugarless Apple Pie 78
Fruit Cocktail Delight. 78
Fruit Gelatin 79
Molasses Cookies 80

Orange Sherbet 81
Pecan Pie 82
Pumpkin Pie with Pecan Topping 83
Strawberry Shortcake 84
Sweet Potato Pie 85
Yellow Cake with Orange Glaze 86

Breads and Pie Crusts **87**
Golden Cornbread 88
Holiday Rolls. 89
Memorable Cornbread Dressing/Stuffing. 90
Pie Crust. 91
Pizza Crust. 91
Walnut Raisin Muffins 92
Whole Wheat Bread 93
Whole Wheat Pie Crust 94

Toppings and Fillings **95**
Cream Topping 96
Lasagna Tofu-style Filling. 97
Orange Glaze. 98
Pecan Crumble Topping 99
Strawberry Filling 100

My Seven Favorite Menus **101**
Planning a Meal. 101

Additional Tips for Maintaining Good Health **103**
Success Stories **108**
Stock Your Pantry **110**
Bibliography **112**
About the Author. **113**
Alphabetical Recipe Index **114**

Introduction

I recently read an excerpt from Darren McGrady's book, *Eating Royally* (2007, p. 57, 58), in which he writes of his many years of service as head chef to the Queen of England and her family. Upon retirement, he detailed his experience.

"The Queen," he writes, "has many duties to perform—although none are more important than planning the family's food and menus." Imagine Queen Elizabeth and her staff planning the menus a year in advance. It's hard for me to plan a day in advance, let alone a year!

These meals are planned in great detail. There is a specific mealtime scheduled, and they eat simple foods when they are in season. Fresh fruits, vegetables, and whole grains appear on their table with the remainder of the meal. There's even a food budget: All fresh ingredients are bought at discounted prices.

All this reflects the Queen's knowledge in caring for the members of her home. She knows that wonderful-tasting food, served attractively, and of superior quality, puts family and guests at ease.

One of my favorite authors, Ellen G. White, writes, "It is the right of every daughter of Eve to have a thorough knowledge of household duties…. She may preside as a queen in her own domain. It is her right to understand the mechanism of the human body [how it works] and the principles of hygiene, the matters of diet and dress, labor and recreation, and countless others that intimately concern the well-being of her household" (1952, p. 87).

She continues, "To the health and happiness of the whole family nothing is more vital than skill and intelligence on the part of the cook. By ill-prepared, unwholesome food may hinder and even ruin both the adult's usefulness and the child's development…. By providing food adapted to the needs of the body, and at the same time inviting and palatable, she can accomplish as much in the right as otherwise she accomplishes in the wrong direction" (1952, p. 89).

I wrote this book a few years ago, reluctantly questioning whether it was relevant for the time, so the manuscript was filed away and forgotten. Since then, the state of America's health has been declining rapidly, forcing me to take a second look. It now seems timelier than ever.

I retrieved the material from my files, dusted it off, tweaked it here and there, and I share it now with you. You will find this book to be revolutionary, easy, and fun, if put into practice.

Today more than 60 percent of adults and children are overweight (10 to 19 percent above ideal weight) or obese (20 percent or more above ideal weight), and these figures continue to rise each year. It behooves each of us to take a serious look at how we can turn these statistics around. Nutrition experts have encouraged us to add more fruits, vegetables, whole grains, and nuts to our diet, and to cut back on fats, sugar, and salt. This is precisely what *Dinner at a Queen's Table* advocates.

Bringing families back to their own dinner tables is another goal of mine. Columbia University conducted a study on families who planned, prepared, and ate dinner at home. They concluded that children formed better relationships with their parents when they ate together. The research also indicated that teens between the ages of sixteen and eighteen who ate at their own dinner table with the family at least five times a week were significantly less likely to get involved in drugs, they did better in school, and they formed stronger friendships (CASAColumbia 2012).

I also felt compelled to publish now as I noticed that most plant-based cookbooks today start at a more advanced level of cooking, which can discourage participation in the long run because it's hard to jump from one to ten overnight. As a health educator and cooking school instructor, travelling throughout the country, I've learned that people want to start at a place of familiarity. Taste buds must adapt to a new way of eating, and *Dinner at a Queen's Table* is written with the beginner in mind.

This cookbook contains transitional recipes. This lifestyle change toward plant-based living is progressive. Start with one plant-based meal a week and add a second meal when you feel comfortable. Before long, by taking small steps, you and your family will experience a marked difference in health; you'll have more energy, look younger, and you'll want to move on to the next step.

I've also included a section called "My Seven Favorite Menus," illustrating how easy it is to get started. A good idea for saving time is to double or even triple a recipe you like and freeze it for future meals; then you may only need to add a salad and you already have your next meal ready! (Incidentally, adding a raw green salad as often as possible helps the body obtain some of the necessary live enzymes it craves.)

All recipes have nutritional facts that illustrate how they are low-fat, low-salt, low-sugar, and without cholesterol or trans-fats. Trans-fats are known to clog the arteries, leading to many of the lifestyle diseases today such as heart disease, diabetes, hypertension, some cancers, and strokes. These are a few from a long list of ailments related to lifestyle.

The margarine or spreads used in my recipes contain no trans-fats. Most local supermarkets carry several brands: Earth Balance® and Smart Balance® are two commonly used healthy spreads. Extra virgin olive oil will be our primary oil in cooking, since it doesn't clog the arteries, followed by canola oil, which provides a lighter taste when baking.

The U.S. Department of Agriculture has attempted to make it easier for us to select better meal choices by discarding the old food pyramid and creating a new one, "My Plate," to guide us with our portions. They recommend you eat more vegetables (builders of the blood) than fruits (cleansers of the blood), more whole grains than proteins, and a little dairy on the side (USDA, https://www.myplate.gov/ [accessed April 17, 2021]). Today most supermarkets carry a wide variety of alternatives to dairy: soy milk, rice milk, and almond milk are all fortified with extra calcium and help in controlling cholesterol.

In the back of this book are seven additional health tips, and when implemented together, they have contributed to longer life. Health researchers have travelled the world searching for the healthiest people. Epidemiologists located several groups: one in a small village in Italy, another in Japan, and the third in the United States. Each group was featured in the November 2005 edition of *National Geographic*, entitled "The Secrets of Living Longer" (Buettner). Interestingly, all the groups' health practices were similar; however, in the United States they scored much higher. What made the difference, it seems, is that they don't smoke or drink alcohol, and they go to church. Additionally, spending time in service to others seems to add extra energetic years to their lives. This group is said to live seven to ten years beyond the general population.

My cookbook has implemented the general principles compiled from these groups and I've come up with creative and delicious recipes to reflect these health practices. You'll also find supplemental information to complete the picture of healthy living.

Entrees

Every other dish in a menu is selected in relation to this main dish.
It is the principle attraction.

Baked Macaroni and Cheese

1 (8-ounce) package whole grain elbow macaroni
2 tablespoons Smart Balance® margarine
1 tablespoon nutritional yeast
½ teaspoon sea salt
⅛ teaspoon onion powder
2 ½ cups soy milk
2 tablespoons soy sour cream
4 cups soy yellow cheddar cheese, grated and divided

***

Preheat oven to 375 degrees.
Cook macaroni as label directs, then drain.
Melt margarine in skillet. Add macaroni, yeast, salt, and onion powder.
Pour in milk. Add sour cream and ½ of cheese. Mix well.
Pour mixture into greased 9 x 13 baking dish, sprinkling remaining cheese on top.
Cover with aluminum foil. Bake for 20 to 25 minutes, or until golden brown.
Yield: Serves 8

Nutrition Information:

Single serving: 162 calories; 7 grams total fat; 537 mg sodium; 157 mg potassium; 16 grams carbohydrates; 3 grams fiber; 1 gram sugar; 12 grams protein

Baked Tofu

2 large cakes firm tofu, sliced
1 tablespoon onion powder
1 teaspoon garlic powder

¼ cup Bragg® All Purpose Seasoning
2 cups Italian breadcrumbs
Olive oil spray

***

Marinate tofu in refrigerator overnight, in glass or plastic container, with onion powder, garlic powder, and All-Purpose Seasoning.
Preheat oven to 375 degrees.
Drain, then transfer to plastic bag filled with the breadcrumbs. Shake vigorously to coat both sides with crumbs.
Spray pans with olive oil and place tofu in single layer.
Bake for 30 minutes, or until light brown.
Yield: Serves 10

Nutrition Information:

Single serving: 144 calories; 7 grams total fat; 0 mg cholesterol; 475 mg sodium; 166 mg potassium; 19.6 grams carbohydrates; 13 grams protein

Barbecue Tofu

3 large cakes extra firm tofu, large slices
1 ½ teaspoon onion powder
½ teaspoon garlic powder
Olive oil spray
2 cups barbecue sauce:
3 cups tomato sauce

1 cup honey
1 tablespoon onion powder
1 tablespoon garlic power
2 tablespoons Bragg All Purpose Seasoning®
1 tablespoon sweet basil
2 tablespoons lemon juice

***

Preheat oven to 350 degrees.
Add all ingredients in medium-sized pot. Simmer for 20 minutes, covered.
Spray pans with olive oil. Add single layer of tofu.
Bake for 20 minutes.
Brush tofu slices with barbecue sauce. Bake for 15 minutes. Turn slices over and brush with sauce.
Bake 10 minutes more.
Serve this tasty protein entrée with any vegetable.
Yield: Serves 10

Nutrition Information:

Single serving: 147 calories; 0 grams total fat; 0 mg cholesterol; 558 mg sodium; 38 grams carbohydrates; 1 gram fiber; 30 grams sugar; 2 grams protein

Cabbage Rolls

12 whole cabbage leaves
Olive oil
1 can vegeburger or 1 package Yves® vegetarian burger
1 cup brown rice, cooked
1 egg, or equivalent egg substitute
1 medium onion, diced

¼ cup celery, diced
1 teaspoon chicken-style seasoning
1 teaspoon sweet basil
½ cup tofu sour cream
1 cup tomato sauce
Tofu cheese (optional)

***

Preheat oven to 350 degrees.
Steam cabbage leaves in boiling water until soft and bright green.
In skillet, add olive oil, burger, onions and celery. Sauté until burger and vegetables are brown. Add brown rice, chicken-style seasoning, sweet basil, sour cream, tomato sauce, and egg or egg substitute. Mix well.
Spoon 1 to 2 tablespoons of mixture into center of cabbage leaves.
Roll leaves tightly around mixture, folding in sides as you roll.
Place each roll seam-side down into a greased, flat baking dish and cover with tomato sauce.
Cover dish with aluminum foil and bake for 45 minutes.
Optional: Cover with tofu cheese 10 minutes before serving.
Yield: Serves 12

Nutrition Information:

Single serving: 53 calories; 0.8 grams total fat; 0.2 grams saturated fat; 1.3 mg cholesterol; 229 mg sodium; 206 mg potassium; 9 grams carbohydrates; 2.8 grams protein (Vegeburger nutrition information not included)

Choplets® Loaf

4 tablespoons Smart Balance® margarine
1 cup onions, chopped
1 cup mushrooms, sliced
½ teaspoon sage
1 can Choplets®, ground
1 cup raw potatoes, shredded
3 eggs or equivalent egg substitute
¼ teaspoon thyme

***

Preheat oven to 350 degrees.
Sauté onions and mushrooms in margarine until soft.
In large bowl, mix sage, Choplets®, potatoes, eggs, and thyme. Mix well.
Bake in greased baking pan for 1 hour. Done when center springs back at the touch.
Yield: Serves 10

Nutrition Information:

Single serving: 64 calories; 4 grams total fat; 96 mg sodium; 102 mg potassium; 5 grams carbohydrates; 3 grams protein

Delectable Vegetable Stew

1 tablespoon cornstarch
1-2 tablespoons cold water
1 medium zucchini, sliced
2 cups green beans, frozen
2 stalks celery, sliced

1 teaspoon sea salt
1 small onion, sliced
2 teaspoons liquid smoke
1 large (15-ounce) can diced tomatoes, undrained
1 cup water

***

Smooth cornstarch into cold water.
In medium saucepan, combine all remaining ingredients with cornstarch mixture. Bring to a boil.
Reduce heat. Simmer, covered, for 40 minutes or until tender.
Serve hot.
Yield: Serves 6

Nutrition Information:
Single serving: 14 calories; 0 grams total fat; 410 mg sodium; 3 grams carbohydrates; 1gram fiber

Haystacks Combo

2 large bags corn chips
Pinto Beans (excluding brown rice) recipe (p. 21) or 2 (28-ounce) cans kidney beans, heated and seasoned with onions and garlic
1 medium onion, chopped
1 large head of green leaf lettuce
4 tomatoes, diced
2 cans black olives, sliced
1 large jar of salsa
Creamy Italian dressing
2 cups tofu cheese, grated

***

On individual plates, start with layer of chips.
Add a layer of beans and sprinkle with onions.
Follow with layer of lettuce; then add tomatoes, olives, salsa, and dressing.
Top with cheese.
This is a complete meal.
Yield: Serves 10

Nutrition Information:

Single serving: 10 calories; 0 grams total fat; 5 mg sodium; 2 grams carbohydrates; 1 gram fiber (Canned beans, corn chips, and salsa nutrition information not included)

Lasagna

1 recipe Spaghetti Sauce (p. 24), divided
1 box lasagna noodles, uncooked and divided
1 recipe Tofu Style Filling divided (p. 97)
1 cup yellow soy cheese, grated

***

Preheat oven to 350 degrees.
In 9 x 13 pan, add thin layer (about ⅓ total amount) of Spaghetti Sauce.
Continue with a layer of noodles, then a layer of tofu filling.
Add, in same order, another layer using half the remaining tomato sauce, noodles, and remaining tofu.
End with the remaining tomato sauce. Top with cheese.
Cover with aluminum foil.
Bake for 1 hour. Allow to cool and set. Warm at 350 for 10 minutes.
Yield: Serves 12

Nutrition Information:

Single serving: 274 calories; 2 grams total fat; 336 mg sodium;10 grams carbohydrates; 12 grams sugar; 10 grams fiber; 2 grams protein

Low-cal Chili

3 ½ cups kidney beans, soaked
2 cups vegeburger
1 medium onion, chopped
4 stalks celery, sliced
½ cup red bell pepper, chopped
Olive oil
6 cups warm water
3 cups diced tomatoes, undrained
2 teaspoons chili powder
1 teaspoon sweet basil

***

Wash kidney beans and soak overnight in water. Discard water after use.
Sauté burger, onion, celery, and bell pepper in oil.
In large pot, combine beans, warm water, sautéed vegetables, and tomatoes (with liquid). Stir together, then add remaining ingredients.
Cover and simmer for 45 minutes.
Yield: Serves 10

Nutrition Information:

Single serving: 209 calories; 6 grams total fat; 376 mg sodium; 514 mg potassium; 21 grams carbohydrates; 6 grams protein (Does not include vegeburger nutrition information)

Pecan Meatballs

1 cup pecans, ground
½ cup raw sunflower seeds, ground
1 onion, chopped
3 cloves garlic, minced
½ cup green onion, chopped

2 cups breadcrumbs
2 cups tofu cheese, grated
3 large eggs, or equivalent egg substitute
1 teaspoon sea salt
Olive oil spray

***

Preheat oven to 350 degrees.
Mix all ingredients in large bowl.
Shape into meatballs (¼ cup each) by hand.
Bake in greased pan until brown.
Put patties in sauce when used with spaghetti.
Yield: 24 meatballs

Nutrition Information:

Single serving: 171 calories; 10 grams total fat; 1gram saturated fat; 0.5 mg cholesterol; 243 mg sodium; 269 mg potassium; 13 grams carbohydrates; 7.4 grams protein

Pinto Beans and Brown Rice

1 pound dry pinto beans
1 large onion, chopped
4 cloves garlic, minced
½ cup red bell pepper, chopped
2 stalks celery, chopped
1 package BOCA® breakfast patties, ground (or your favorite meatless patties)
Flaky Brown Rice recipe (see p. 64)

***

Discard any unwanted beans and materials.
Wash beans well and soak overnight in refrigerator, with enough water to cover the beans.
Rinse beans thoroughly.
Combine all ingredients in large pot, adding enough warm water to cover beans by 2 inches. Cook over medium-high heat for 90 minutes, or until beans are soft and gravy thickens.
Serve alongside or over brown rice.
Yield: Serves 10

Nutrition Information:

Single serving: 61 calories; 0 grams total fat; 22 mg sodium; 16 grams carbohydrates; 12 grams fiber; 7 grams protein (Boca patties nutrition information not included)

Rolled Oat Patties

1 large onion, chopped
½ cup celery, chopped
1 cup quick oats
½ cup breadcrumbs
1 cup brown rice, cooked
1 teaspoon nutritional yeast flakes
1 teaspoon McKay's® Chicken Style Seasoning
2 eggs, or equivalent egg substitute
Olive oil
Rolled Oat Patties Broth (p. 60)
1 can cream of mushroom soup

***

Preheat oven to 375 degrees.
Sauté onions and celery in oil until soft.
In separate bowl, combine remaining ingredients, except for mushroom soup. Add sautéed onions and celery, and mix.
Form patties and brown lightly in oil.
Bring broth to a boil. Drop patties into broth and simmer for 15 minutes.
Remove patties from broth (retaining broth) and arrange in greased, flat casserole pan.
Mix broth with cream of mushroom soup and pour over patties.
Bake for 30 minutes.
Yield: Serves 8

Nutrition Information:

Single serving: 154 calories; 2 grams total fat; 115 mg sodium; 31 grams carbohydrates; 3 grams fiber; 4 grams protein

Sausage and Noodle Casserole

1 medium onion, chopped
2 stalks celery, chopped
4 cloves garlic, minced
½ cup red bell pepper, chopped
Olive oil
2 (15-ounce) cans tomato sauce
1 tablespoon turbinado sugar
1 package Morningstar Farms® Breakfast Patties, ground
Salt
4 ½ cups wide whole grain noodles, cooked
½ cup tofu cheese, grated
¼ cup paprika
Smart Balance® margarine

***

Preheat oven to 400 degrees.
Sauté onions, celery, garlic, and red bell pepper in small amount of olive oil until soft.
Add tomato sauce, sugar, ground breakfast patties, and salt; stir until well-mixed.
Add noodles and cheese; stir until well-mixed.
Spoon into greased, flat baking dish.
Dot the top with dabs of margarine, then sprinkle paprika on top.
Bake for 45 minutes or until lightly brown and firm in the center.
Yield: Serves 10

Nutrition Information:

Single serving: 97 calories; 1 gram total fat; 17 mg sodium; 19 grams carbohydrates; 1 gram fiber; 2 grams sugar; 5 grams protein

Spaghetti and Pecan Meatballs

Spaghetti Sauce

1 (12-ounce) can tomato paste
1 (28-ounce) can tomatoes, chopped
1 large onion, chopped
2 stalks garlic, chopped
2 tablespoons turbinado sugar
¼ teaspoon Italian seasoning

4 cups water
1 teaspoon sea salt
Pecan Meatballs recipe (p. 20)
1 package whole grain spaghetti

***

Combine all ingredients in large sauce pot; simmer for 1 hour.
In a separate pot, cook spaghetti according to package directions.
Add meatballs to sauce and cook 10 minutes.
Serve over hot spaghetti noodles.
Yield: Serves 10

Nutrition Information:

Single serving: 14 calories; 0 grams total fat; 246 mg sodium; 4 grams carbohydrates; 2 grams sugar; 1 gram protein (Does not include noodle or meatball nutrition information)

Tofu Cheese and Potato Supreme

5 large potatoes, unpeeled
1 cup tofu sour cream
2 cups soy milk
½ teaspoon sea salt
½ teaspoon garlic powder
1 teaspoon onion powder
1 (12-ounce) package tofu cheddar, grated and divided
or 1 ½ cups Nutty Cheese Sauce recipe (p. 58)

***

Preheat oven to 400 degrees.
Wash and scrub potatoes with vegetable brush.
Thinly slice potatoes and place in greased, flat casserole dish.
In small saucepan, combine sour cream, milk, sea salt, garlic powder, and onion powder. Bring to boil.
Add ½ cheese to mixture, cooking until cheese melts.
Pour over potatoes, then top with remaining cheese.
Cover with aluminum foil and bake for 45 minutes, or until tender.
(If using Nutty Cheese Sauce, don't add it to milk mixture—just use to top potatoes.)
Yield: Serves 10

Nutrition Information:

Single serving: 240 calories; 5 grams total fat; 469 mg sodium; 809 mg potassium; 37 grams carbohydrates; 6 grams fiber; 2 grams sugar; 13 grams protein

Vege-links and Baked Beans

1 package Morningstar Farms® breakfast links
2 (15-ounce) cans navy beans
1 tablespoon lemon juice
¼ cup molasses
½ cup ketchup
¼ cup onion, diced

***

Preheat oven to 350 degrees.
Slice links into bite-size pieces.
Combine all ingredients and mix gently.
Pour into greased baking dish.
Bake for 35 minutes until lightly brown.
Yield: Serves 10

Nutrition Information:

Single serving: 220 calories; 4 grams total fat; 305 mg sodium; 18 mg potassium; 32 grams carbohydrates; 10 grams fiber; 8 grams sugar; 15 grams protein

Vegeburger Loaf

1 (19-ounce) can vegan burger, mashed
3 tablespoons Smart Balance® margarine
½ cup onion, chopped
½ cup red bell pepper, chopped
2 stalks celery, chopped
3 eggs or equivalent egg substitute
½ cup sour cream
1 cup cracker crumbs
2 tablespoons parsley flakes
1 teaspoon sweet basil
Tomato sauce

***

Preheat oven to 350 degrees.
Mix all ingredients in large bowl.
Spray loaf pan with olive oil. Shape mixture into pan. Top with tomato sauce.
Bake 45 minutes. Done when firm in center or prick in center with toothpick. If it comes out clean, it is done.
Yield: Serves 10

Nutrition Information:

Single serving: 95 calories; 5 grams total fat; 6 mg cholesterol; 187 mg sodium; 12 grams carbohydrates; 3 grams sugar; 1 gram protein

Wok Vegetable Stir-fry with Tofu

Olive oil
1 packaged extra-firm tofu, cubed
4 cups fresh broccoli, spears
1 cup fresh carrots, sliced
1 medium onion, sliced
4 cloves garlic, minced
1 red bell pepper, chopped coarsely

½ cup snow peas
1 cup tomatoes, wedged
1 cup fresh mushrooms, sliced
Flaky Brown Rice recipe (p. 66)
Ginger Sauce recipe (p. 56)
Sesame seeds for garnish

***

Wash vegetables; set tomatoes aside. Mix remaining vegetables.
Place wok on high heat and coat the bottom and sides with olive oil. Add tofu to brown. Remove tofu.
Add oil to coat wok again; then add vegetable mixture, tossing just until slightly softened, but still firm and crunchy.
Re-coat wok with oil one more time and toss in tomatoes and tofu.
Remove from heat and mix all cooked ingredients together.
Yield: Serves 8

Nutrition Information:

Single serving: 18 calories; 0 grams total fat; 0 mg cholesterol; 19 mg sodium; 1 gram fiber; 0 grams sugar; 2 grams protein

Vegetables

Vegetables add color, texture, and fiber to your meals. It is best to use a wide variety.

Baby Lima Beans and Peas

1 tablespoon olive oil
1 tablespoon flour
2 pounds lima beans, frozen
1 pound green peas, frozen
½ cup green onions, chopped
1 teaspoon sea salt
2 cups warm water

***

Using olive oil, brown flour in pot, whisking rapidly.
Combine other ingredients into pot.
Cook on medium heat until beans are soft but firm.
Serve as a side dish with spaghetti or any entrée.
Yield: Serves 8–10

Nutrition Information:

Single serving: 160 calories; 360 mg sodium; 485 mg potassium; 30 grams carbohydrates; 7 grams fiber; 3 grams sugar; 10 grams protein

Banana and Sweet Potato Soufflé

6 medium-sized sweet potatoes
2 tablespoons vanilla extract (non-alcohol)
¼ cup honey
¼ cup soy milk

1 tablespoon molasses
¼ teaspoon cinnamon, or coriander
4 ripe bananas, mashed

***

Bake, cool, peel, and mash potatoes.
Preheat oven to 350 degrees.
Blend, adding vanilla, honey, milk, molasses, and cinnamon. Mix well.
Place ½ of potatoes in lightly greased casserole dish.
Spread mashed bananas on top of potatoes.
Gently fold remaining potatoes over bananas.
Bake for 30 minutes.
Yield: Serves 8

Nutrition Information:

Single serving: 214 calories; 0.5 grams total fat; 23 mg sodium; 532 mg potassium; 51grams carbohydrates; 5 grams fiber; 18 grams sugar; 3 grams protein

Black-eyed Peas and Okra

2 tablespoons flour
2 pounds black-eyed peas, frozen
1 large onion, chopped
½ cup red bell pepper, diced
4 cloves garlic, chopped
1 large tomato, chopped
1 teaspoon browning sauce
1 teaspoon chicken-style seasoning
1 cup okra, cut and frozen

***

Brown flour in large pot.
Add other ingredients, except okra. Add enough water to cover by 2 inches.
Cook over medium heat for 45 minutes, or until peas are soft but firm, and gravy thickens.
Add okra and cook 10 more minutes.
Yield: Serves 8

Nutrition Information:

Single serving: 123 calories; 0 grams total fat; 8 mg sodium; 171 mg potassium; 6 grams fiber; 3 grams sugar; 5 grams protein

Crunchy Cabbage and Red Bell Pepper

1 medium head of cabbage, sliced in thin strips
Olive oil
1 cup onion, sliced
3 tablespoons Italian dressing
¼ teaspoon sea salt
¼ teaspoon Italian seasoning
½ cup red bell pepper, sliced into thin strips

***

Wash cabbage thoroughly.
In wok or large skillet, add just enough oil to cover the bottom. Add cabbage and onion.
Toss as mixture begins to cook.
Pour in Italian dressing, salt, Italian seasoning, and bell pepper.
Cook until cabbage is tender but not limp.
Note: Children love the crunchy texture!
Yield: Serves 8–10

Nutrition Information:

Single serving: 34 calories; 1 gram total fat; 28 mg sodium; 242 mg potassium; 6 grams carbohydrates; 2 grams fiber; 2 grams protein

Fried Corn

¼ cup olive oil
2 pounds corn, frozen
½ cup onion, chopped
⅓ cup red bell pepper, diced
1 tablespoon unbleached flour
½ teaspoon Italian seasoning

***

Warm oil in skillet and add corn, onion, and bell pepper.
Stir over medium heat for 15 minutes.
Add flour, seasoning, and salt. Cook until tender.
Yield: 8

Nutrition Information:

Single serving: 153 calories; 6 grams total fat; 24 mg sodium; 211 mg potassium; 16 grams carbohydrates; 2 grams fiber; 2 grams sugar; 2 grams protein

Garlic Spinach

3 pounds spinach, fresh
¼ cup olive oil
4 cloves garlic, minced

***

Wash spinach thoroughly.
Add oil to medium pot. Turn in spinach.
Toss for approximately 3 minutes, then remove from heat.
Sprinkle with minced garlic.
Yield: Serves 4

Nutrition Information:

Single serving: 153 calories; 11 grams total fat; 202 mg sodium; 1,435 mg potassium; 10 grams carbohydrates; 6 grams fiber; 1 gram sugar; 8 grams protein

Vegetables 35

Honey Beets

2 (16-ounce) cans sliced beets, drained and liquid retained
2 tablespoons honey
¼ teaspoon sea salt

2 teaspoons cold water.
1 teaspoon cornstarch
2 tablespoon lemon juice
⅔ cup liquid from beets

***

Combine beets, ⅔ cup of retained liquid, honey, and salt in saucepan. Heat thoroughly.
Smooth cornstarch with cold water and add to saucepan.
Cook over medium heat until consistency is even.
Remove from heat; add lemon juice.
Yield: Serves 8

Nutrition Information:

Single serving: 64 calories; 107 mg sodium; 127 mg potassium; 9 grams carbohydrates; 7 grams sugar; 0.7 grams protein

Mixed Greens

1 bunch kale
2 bunches mustard greens
1 small onion, diced
¼ cup olive oil
1 teaspoon chicken-style seasoning

***

Wash greens thoroughly and cut off stems.
Fold a few leaves together at a time and slice.
Place greens in pot. (They should remain fairly moist after washing.)
Add onions, oil, and chicken-style seasoning.
Cook 25 minutes, stirring occasionally, until tender but not mushy.
Yield: Serves 8

Nutrition Information:

Single serving: 146 calories; 7 grams total fat; 33 mg sodium; 379 mg potassium; 8 grams carbohydrates; 4 grams fiber; 1 gram sugar; 3 grams protein

Pan-Browned Potatoes

1 tablespoons olive oil
½ teaspoon sea salt
10 small red potatoes, peeled and cooked
Parsley (dried) or dill for garnish

***

Warm oil in skillet. Add salt; cook and stir until mixture is brown.
Place potatoes in oil, stirring constantly until lightly browned.
Sprinkle with parsley.
Yield: Serves 6

Nutrition Information:

Single serving: 259 calories; 5 grams total fat; 19 mg sodium; 1,209 mg potassium; 50 grams carbohydrates; 6 grams fiber; 2 grams sugar; 6 grams protein

Peas with Sliced Almonds

1 pound green peas, frozen
¼ cup onions, chopped
2 teaspoons Smart Balance® margarine
½ cup tofu sour cream
¼ teaspoon sea salt
¼ cup sliced almonds

***

In medium saucepan, cook peas as directed.
In separate saucepan, sauté onions in margarine, then add sour cream and salt, stirring until smooth.
Pour over peas.
Top with almonds.
Yield: Serves 8

Nutrition Information:

Single serving: 116 calories; 5 grams total fat; 342 mg sodium; 13 grams carbohydrates; 4 grams fiber; 5 grams sugar; 6 grams protein

Savory Cauliflower and Zucchini

1 fresh cauliflower, chopped
½ cup water
1 large zucchini, cubed
¼ cup onion, chopped
1 teaspoon Smart Balance® margarine
1 tomato, wedged
½ cup soy milk
½ teaspoon sea salt
1 cup tofu cheddar cheese, grated

***

Wash cauliflower thoroughly.
Steam in water until slightly soft. Drain.
In medium skillet, sauté zucchini and onion in margarine for 3 minutes. Set aside.
In small saucepan, add milk and salt. Bring to boil, then add cheese. Continue cooking until cheese melts.
Combine all ingredients into skillet. Heat thoroughly.
Top with melted cheese.
Yield: Serves 8

Nutrition Information:

Single serving: 110 calories; 4 grams total fat; 239 mg sodium; 510 mg potassium; 12 grams carbohydrates; 10 grams protein

Twice Baked Sweet Potatoes

8 medium sweet potatoes, unpeeled
¼ cup turbinado sugar
½ cup honey

1 teaspoon vanilla extract, non-alcohol
1 teaspoon almond extract, non-alcohol

***

Preheat oven to 350 degrees.
Bake potatoes until slightly soft. Let cool, then peel and slice.
Place sliced potatoes in greased baking pan.
Combine honey, vanilla extract, and almond extract. Pour mixture over potatoes. Sprinkle sugar on top.
Bake in preheated oven for 10 minutes.
Yield: Serves 10

Nutrition Information:

Single serving: 157 calories; 16 mg sodium; 236 mg potassium; 37 grams carbohydrates; 3 grams fiber; 7 grams sugar; 2 grams protein

Vegetable Platter

Mixed green lettuce
1 (16-ounce) can beets
2 large tomatoes, sliced
Celery sticks
Carrots, sliced into thin strips
Cauliflower, cut in pieces
Broccoli, cut in florets
1 red onion, diced
Marinade for Vegetable Platter recipe (p. 52)

***

Arrange lettuce on large platter.
Top with sections of tomatoes, celery sticks, carrots, cauliflower, and broccoli.
Sprinkle onions over top of vegetables.
Pour marinade over vegetables.
Yield: Serves 10

Nutrition Information:

Single serving: 48 calories; 48 mg sodium; 402 mg potassium; 11 grams carbohydrates; 3 grams fiber; 2 grams sugar; 2 grams protein

Salads

The salad is the only dish that can stand alone as a complete meal and also mix well with other vegetables or fruit.

Best Tossed Salad

1 large head of leaf lettuce
2 carrots, peeled and slivered with a potato peeler
½ sweet onion, sliced thin
1 cup black olives

1 large cucumber, sliced
3 tomatoes, cubed and divided
Homemade Dressings (p. 49)

***

Wash and dry lettuce. Tear into bite-size pieces.
In salad bowl, add a layer of lettuce, carrots, onion, olives, cucumbers, and tomatoes. Repeat with second layer. Garnish top with remainder of tomatoes.
Yield: Serves 10

Nutrition Information:

Single serving: 23 calories; 18 mg sodium; 218 mg potassium; 5 grams carbohydrates; 1 gram fiber; 1 gram sugar; 0.9 grams protein

Carrot and Apple Salad

3 cups carrots, coarsely shredded
3 cups red delicious apples, diced
¼ cup raisins

¼ cup soy milk
Mayonnaise (or Vegenaise®)

***

Combine carrots, apples, raisins, and milk in large bowl.
Toss with mayonnaise to taste.
Refrigerate until ready to serve.
Yield: Serves 10

Nutrition Information:

Single serving: 83 calories; 0.5 grams total fat; 31 mg sodium; 273 mg potassium; 21 grams carbohydrates; 3 grams fiber; 10 grams sugar; 1.4 grams protein

Layered Salad

1 head romaine lettuce, torn into bite-size pieces
2 cups cauliflower, sliced
4 green onions, sliced
1 cup carrots, grated
1 cup broccoli, sliced
2 tomatoes, chopped
Nacho cheese-flavored chips, crumbled
Creamy Italian dressing

***

Mix first 6 ingredients in large bowl, in order given.
Use only enough Italian dressing to coat the mixture.
Top with nacho cheese-flavored chips, crumbled.
Yield: Serves 10

Nutrition Information:

Single serving: 221 calories; 2 grams total fat; 206 mg sodium; 239.4 mg potassium; 50 grams carbohydrates; 17 grams fiber; 7 grams sugar; 12 grams protein

Macaroni Salad

3 cups whole grain elbow macaroni, cooked
1 tablespoon olive oil, extra virgin
⅓ cup onion, chopped fine
½ cup celery, chopped
⅓ cup red bell pepper
1 cup green peas, frozen
4-ounce jar pimentos, drained
¼ cup lemon juice
1 teaspoon sea salt
1 teaspoon chicken-style seasoning
Mayonnaise (or Vegenaise®)
Lettuce leaves

***

Cook macaroni according to package instructions. Drain.
Drizzle olive oil over macaroni and let cool.
Combine cooled macaroni in bowl with remaining ingredients.
Toss with mayonnaise to taste. Serve on lettuce leaves.
Yield: Serves 12

Nutrition Information:

Single serving: 146 calories; 2 grams total fat; 19 mg sodium; 62 mg potassium; 31 grams carbohydrates; 5 grams fiber; 1 gram sugar; 5 grams protein

Mixed Fruit Salad

2 cups fresh strawberries, halved
1 small pineapple, pared and cubed
2 kiwi fruit, sliced

Honey Sesame Dressing recipe (p. 51):
2 tablespoons olive oil
2 tablespoons honey
1 tablespoon lemon juice
1 teaspoon sesame seeds

***

Mix fruit in bowl. Pour Honey Sesame Dressing ingredients in bottle. Shake well. Add to fruit and mix well.
Yield: Serves 6

Nutrition Information:
Single serving: 72 calories; 3 mg sodium; 274 mg potassium; 18 grams carbohydrates; 3 grams fiber; 11 grams sugar

Potato Salad

6 large baking potatoes, washed, peeled, and diced
¼ cup onion, diced
½ cup red bell pepper, diced
¼ cup kosher relish (dill or sweet)
1 tablespoon lemon juice
1 (4-ounce) jar pimentos, drained
¼ teaspoon Italian seasoning
1 teaspoon sea salt
Mayonnaise (or Vegenaise®)
Paprika
2 tomatoes, sliced thick

***

In large pot, add potatoes. Add water until potatoes are covered by 2 inches.
Cook for 40 minutes, until slightly soft, then drain and let cool.
Place potatoes in large bowl with remaining ingredients.
Toss with mayonnaise to taste.
Sprinkle with paprika and garnish with tomatoes.
Yield: Serves 10

Nutrition Information:

Single serving: 179 calories; 0 grams total fat; 37 mg sodium; 1,001 mg potassium; 41 grams carbohydrates; 5 grams fiber; 2 grams sugar; 5 grams protein

Taco Salad

3 cups lettuce, chopped
2 cups tomatoes, diced
½ cup green onions, chopped
1 (16-ounce) can barbeque pinto beans
½ cup tofu cheese, grated
Creamy Italian dressing
Nacho cheese-flavored tortilla chips, crumbled

***

Mix lettuce, tomatoes, onion, pinto beans, cheese, and Italian dressing in large bowl.
Use only enough Italian dressing to coat mixture.
Top with chip crumbs.
Yield: Serves 10

Nutrition Information:

Single serving: 202 calories; 9 grams total fat; 473 mg sodium; 187 mg potassium; 26 grams carbohydrates; 2 grams fiber; 7 grams protein

Tomato and Cucumber Salad

3 cups tomatoes, diced
3 cucumbers, diced
½ onions, diced
1 teaspoon Italian seasoning

2 tablespoons lemon juice
1 tablespoon honey
½ cup sweet bell pepper, chopped
1 cup black olives, chopped

***

In large bowl, combine tomatoes, cucumbers, onions, Italian seasoning, bell pepper, and olives. Pour in lemon juice and honey. Toss.
Chill until ready to serve.
Yield: Serves 8

Nutrition Information:

Single serving: 45 calories; 1 gram total fat; 50 mg sodium; 306 mg potassium; 9 grams carbohydrates; 2 grams fiber; 4 grams sugar; 1 gram protein

Vegetable and Spaghetti Salad

1 (8-ounce) box whole grain thin spaghetti, broken into 2-inch pieces
1 tablespoon olive oil
2 cups frozen corn, cooked
2 cups frozen lima beans, cooked
2 medium tomatoes, diced
¾ cup green onions, chopped
⅓ cup fresh parsley
1 teaspoon chicken-style seasoning
Vegetable and Spaghetti Salad Dressing recipe (p. 53)

***

Cook spaghetti according to package directions. Rinse in cold water and drain.
Place drained spaghetti in large bowl and toss with oil.
Add corn, lima beans, tomatoes, green onions, parsley, seasoning, and Vegetable Spaghetti Salad Dressing recipe. Toss and serve.
Yield: Serves 12

Nutrition Information:

Single serving: 145 calories; 2 grams total fat; 15 mg sodium; 338 mg potassium; 7 grams fiber; 1 gram sugar; 6 grams protein

Salad Dressings

Salad dressings can be a low-fat, delicious way to add spice to a salad.

Celery Dressing

1 cup raw cashews, rinsed
2 stalks celery
2 fresh lemons, juiced
5 tablespoons honey

1 tablespoon onion powder
1 teaspoon sea salt
1 cup water

***

Combine all ingredients in blender, blending until smooth.
Refrigerate.
Yield: Serves 10

Nutrition Information:

Single serving: 119 calories; 6 grams total fat; 15 grams sodium; 157 mg potassium; 16 grams carbohydrates; 2 grams fiber; 10 grams sugar; 3 grams protein

Cucumber Dressing

1 cup cashews, raw, rinsed
1 medium cucumber, chopped
4 tablespoons lemon juice
2 tablespoons honey

1 tablespoon onion powder
1 teaspoon garlic powder
1 teaspoon sea salt
⅓ cup water

***

Yield: Serves 8
Combine all ingredients in a blender, blending until smooth.
Refrigerate overnight to thicken.

Nutrition Information:

Single serving: 100 calories; 6 grams total fat; 3 mg sodium; 0 grams carbohydrates; 131 mg potassium; 0 grams fiber; 0 grams protein

Honey Sesame Dressing

2 tablespoons olive oil
2 tablespoons honey
1 tablespoon fresh lemon juice
1 teaspoon sesame seeds

***

Shake all ingredients in container or bottle.
Refrigerate 2 hours.
Pour over Mixed Fruit Salad recipe (p. 45).
Yield: Serves 8

Nutrition Information:

Single serving: 70 calories; 6 grams total fat; 1 mg sodium; 13 mg potassium; 6 grams carbohydrates; 6 grams sugar; 0.3 grams protein

Lip-smacking French Dressing

1 cup raw sunflower seeds
1 (6-ounce) can tomato paste
1 cup water
½ cup honey
½ cup lemon juice
1 teaspoon onion powder
½ teaspoon garlic powder

***

Yield: Serves 12
Combine all ingredients in blender, blending until smooth and creamy.
Refrigerate.

Nutrition Information:

Single serving: 125 calories; 5 grams total fat; 115 mg sodium; 257 mg potassium; 19 grams carbohydrates; 2 grams fiber; 15 grams sugar; 3 grams protein

Marinade for Vegetable Platter

1 cup water
⅓ cup lemon juice
1 tablespoon olive oil
1 tablespoon onion powder

½ teaspoon garlic powder
¼ teaspoon sea salt
½ teaspoon paprika

***

Combine all ingredients in glass bowl or bottle.
Cover and refrigerate overnight.
Pour over vegetables just before serving.
Yield: Serves 7

Nutrition Information:

Single serving: 26 calories; 2 grams total fat; 0 grams sodium; 36 mg potassium; 2 grams carbohydrates; 0 grams fiber; 0.3 grams protein

Vegetable and Spaghetti Salad Dressing

⅓ cup olive oil
5 tablespoons lemon juice
1 teaspoon turbinado sugar

1 teaspoon sea salt
¼ teaspoon paprika
Dash of Italian seasoning

***

In small bowl, whip dressing ingredients.
Pour over spaghetti or vegetable mixture, then toss gently.
Serve immediately, or chill.
Yield: Serves 12

Nutrition Information:

Single serving: 33 calories; 3 grams total fat; 1 mg sodium; 7 mg potassium; 0 grams carbohydrates; 0 grams fiber; 0 grams protein

Sauces, Gravies, and Broth

Sauces, gravies, and broth are terrific ways to add both moisture and flavor.

Easy Brown Gravy

½ cup raw cashews, rinsed
½ cup water
1 teaspoon browning sauce (Gravy Master® Seasoning and Browning Sauce, for example)
1 teaspoon onion powder
1 teaspoon garlic powder
1 teaspoon McKay's® Beef Style Seasoning

***

Blend cashews in water until smooth. Pour into small saucepan and add remaining ingredients. Simmer over medium heat until gravy thickens.
Serve with mashed potatoes, meatless loaves, or rice.
Yield: Serves 8

Nutrition Information:

Single serving: 7 calories; 0 grams total fat; 1 mg sodium; 0 mg potassium; 1 gram carbohydrates; 0 grams fiber; 0 grams protein

Ginger Sauce

3 cups water
2 teaspoons Bragg® Liquid Aminos All Purpose Seasoning
1 tablespoon cornstarch
1 teaspoon onion powder
½ teaspoon garlic powder
1 dash browning sauce
Sea salt to taste
1 pinch fresh ginger, grated

***

In medium saucepan, combine all ingredients, except ginger, and stir over medium heat until sauce thickens. Remove from heat and add ginger.
Serve over rice and stir-fry vegetables.
Yield: Serves 8

Nutrition Information:

Single serving: 22 calories; 0 grams total fat; 135 mg sodium; 0 grams potassium; 5 grams carbohydrates; 0 grams fiber; 0 grams protein

Mom's Brown Gravy

½ cup onion, diced
2 stalks celery, diced
2 cloves garlic, chopped
Olive oil
½ cup unbleached flour
2 teaspoon McKay's® Beef Style Seasoning
4 cups water

***

Sauté onions, celery, and garlic, using minimal oil, until tender. Add flour and let brown.
Transfer mixture into a small saucepan and add seasoning and water. Cook on low heat for 15 minutes, or until thick.
Yield: 4 cups

Nutrition Information:

Single serving: 46 calories; 2 grams total fat; 12 mg sodium; 0 grams potassium; 7 grams carbohydrates; 0 grams fiber; 1 gram protein

Nutty Yellow Cheese Sauce

(While the fat content may seem high, remember that it's mostly mono- and poly-unsaturated, healthy fat!)

1 cup water
½ cup cashews, raw
½ cup sesame seeds, unhulled
⅓ cup nutritional yeast flakes
¼ cup plain pimentos, drained

1 teaspoon onion powder
½ teaspoon garlic powder
3 tablespoons lemon juice
1 teaspoon sea salt
1 pinch turmeric, ground

***

Wash cashews and sesame seeds.
Blend all ingredients until smooth and creamy.
Cover and store in refrigerator until needed.
Use as dip or in other dishes requiring cheese.
Yield: Serves 16

Nutrition Information:

Single serving: 4 calories; 8.3 grams total fat; 236 mg sodium; 1 gram carbohydrate

Pizza Sauce

1 cup tomato sauce
⅛ teaspoon garlic powder
⅛ teaspoon onion powder
⅓ teaspoon Italian seasoning

***

Combine ingredients and spread pizza sauce over crust.
Bake as directed in the Make It Your Way Pizza recipe (p. 70).
Yield: Serves 8

Nutrition Information:

Single serving: 8 calories; 0 grams total fat; 185 mg sodium; 0 g potassium; 2 grams carbohydrates; 2 grams sugar; 0 grams fiber; 0 grams protein

Rolled Oat Patty Broth

2 cups hot water
1 tablespoon browning sauce
1 tablespoon soy sauce, or Bragg® All Purpose Seasoning

***

Combine ingredients in pot. Simmer for 15 minutes.
Yield: Serves 8

Nutrition Information:

Single serving: 2 calories; 0 grams total fat; 68 mg sodium; 0 grams potassium; 0 grams carbohydrates; 0 grams fiber; 0 grams protein; less than 1 gram sugar

Side Dishes

Baked French Fries

A delicious, low-fat recipe. You can have your fries without the extra fat! Kids love them, too.

8 large baking potatoes, peeled
1 tablespoon olive oil
Garlic powder
Sweet basil
Sea salt

***

Wash, peel, and slice potatoes. Cut into sticks.
Toss potatoes with olive oil and sprinkle with garlic powder, sweet basil, and sea salt.
Spray cookie sheet with non-stick oil. Add potato strips in single layer.
Bake at 375° for 45–50 minutes, until golden brown. Serve hot.
Yield: Serves 8

Nutrition Information:

Single serving: 22 calories; 2 grams total fat; 295 mg sodium; 631.6 mg potassium; 2 grams carbohydrates; 2.3 grams fiber; 3 grams protein; 2.6 grams sugar

Broccoli Rice

1 onion, chopped
½ cup Smart Balance® margarine
1 (1-pound bag) frozen broccoli, cooked
1 cup soy yellow cheddar cheese
1 can cream of celery soup
1 cup water
½ cup soy milk
1 cup brown rice, cooked

***

Preheat oven to 350 degrees.
Sauté onions in margarine until soft.
Cook broccoli in separate pot, with just enough water to steam.
When tender, drain and mix with onions. Add remaining ingredients.
Place in greased casserole dish. Bake for 25 minutes.
Yield: Serves 10

Nutrition Information:

Single serving: 104 calories; 7 grams total fat; 259 mg sodium; 70 mg potassium; 8 grams carbohydrates; 0.8 grams fiber; 0.1 grams sugar; 2 grams protein

Cool Banana and Cherry Drink

1 (12-ounce) can cherry juice concentrate, frozen
4 ripe bananas
3 tablespoons honey
2 cups soy milk

***

Mix cherry juice according to can instructions.
Blend bananas, honey, and milk in blender. Add to cherry juice.
Chill. Stir before serving.
Yield: Serves 10

Nutrition Information:

Single serving: 241 calories; 7 grams total fat; 240 mg sodium; 207.9 mg potassium; 23 grams carbohydrates; 2 grams fiber; 11 grams sugar; 12 grams protein

Easy Vegetable Soup

2 cups corn, frozen
2 cups sweet peas
2 stalks celery, chopped
1 medium onion, chopped
1 large can tomato sauce

1 large can tomatoes, undrained
3 cloves garlic, crushed
1 cup whole grain elbow macaroni
2 cups water
Cilantro, minced

***

Combine all ingredients in large pot.
Simmer 35–45 minutes, or until vegetables become tender and water cooks down.
Yield: Serves 10

Nutrition Information:

Single serving: 156 calories; 0 grams total fat; 325 mg sodium; 378 mg potassium; 34 grams carbohydrates; 5 grams fiber; 5 grams sugar; 6 grams protein

Excellent Sandwich Spread

1 can Worthington Linketts®, ground
2 stalks celery, finely diced
1 small onion, chopped
¼ cup sweet pickle relish (kosher)
1 tablespoon lemon juice
1 drop liquid smoke
Mayonnaise (or Vegenaise®)

***

Mix all ingredients in a bowl.
Add mayonnaise to taste.
Spread on crackers or make a sandwich with whole grain bread.
Yield: Serves 10

Nutrition Information:

Single serving: 23 calories; 0.4 grams total fat; 124 mg potassium; less than 1 gram carbohydrates; 0.3 grams fiber; 2 grams sugar; 0.8 grams protein. (Worthington Linkett® nutrition information not included)

Flaky Brown Rice

2 teaspoons olive oil
3 cups brown rice
½ teaspoon sea salt
6 cups water

***

Combine oil, rice, and salt in skillet. Cook, stirring, for 10 minutes.
Add to the water in a medium pot and bring to boil.
Reduce heat to medium. Cook for 1 hour, or until water absorbs and rice is flaky.
Serving: Serve as a side dish to any entree.
Yield: Serves 10

Nutrition Information:

Single serving: 77 calories; 2 grams total fat; 0.3 grams saturated fat; 0 mg cholesterol; 6 mg sodium; 25 mg potassium; 13 grams carbohydrates; 1 gram fiber; 2 grams protein

Fruit Drink

2 cups berry punch
3 cups pineapple juice
½ cup lime juice
Ice (optional)

***

Prepare punch and pineapple juice according to can directions.
Add lime juice and mix well.
Add ice and serve.
Yield: Serves 8

Nutrition Information:

Single serving: 180 calories; 30 mg sodium; 45 grams carbohydrates; 38 grams sugar; 2 grams protein

Fruit Pizza

1 double pizza crust or large crust shaped in pizza pan, or store-bought pizza dough
2 cups ripe fresh fruit (strawberries, peaches, blueberries, pineapple, or kiwi, or combination)
¼ cup turbinado sugar
2 tablespoons cornstarch
2 cups fruit juice

***

Prepare and bake pie crust according to instructions. Let cool.
Ready fruit. Slice strawberries, peaches, etc. Arrange on crust.
Combine sugar, cornstarch, and fruit juice in small saucepan. Cook until thick.
Pour over fruit, then chill for 2 hours.
Slice and serve with milk or fruit drink.
Yield: Serves 8

Nutrition Information:

Single serving: 198 calories; 0 grams total fat; 20 mg sodium; 50 grams carbohydrates; 40 grams sugar; 1 gram protein (Crust nutrition information not included)

Hearty Trail Mix

¾ cup roasted peanuts
1 cup roasted sunflower seeds
1 cup roasted cashews
1 cup raisins

***

Combine ingredients in bowl and serve!
Yield: Serves 10

Nutrition Information:

Single serving: 288 calories; 20 grams total fat; 5 mg sodium; 406 mg potassium; 24 grams carbohydrates; 4 grams fiber; 11 grams sugar; 9 grams protein

Make It Your Way Pizza

Preheat oven to 400 degrees.
Pizza dough of your choice, shaped in pizza pan
Pizza Sauce recipe (p. 59)
Red and yellow bell peppers, sliced thin
Soy patties, crumbled, or soy links, sliced
Soy cheese, cheddar style, grated
Onion, chopped

***

Spread pizza sauce over crust.
Add sausage, vegetables, and cheese.
Bake at 400° until cheese bubbles. Serve hot!
Yield: Serves 8

Nutrition Information:

Single serving: 82 calories; 3 grams total fat; 229 mg sodium; 76 mg potassium; 5 grams carbohydrates; 2 grams fiber; 0 grams sugar; 8 grams protein

Scrambled Tofu

Can be great, cholesterol-free substitute for eggs!

½ cup red bell pepper, chopped
3 green onions, chopped
3 tablespoons olive oil
1 block firm tofu, drained and crumbled
1 tablespoon nutritional yeast
1 teaspoon McKay's® Chicken Style Seasoning
¼ teaspoon turmeric

***

Sauté bell pepper and onions in a small amount of water until soft.
Add oil and remaining ingredients and cook 15 minutes.
Serve in wraps or pitas.
Yield: Serves 8

Nutrition Information:

Single serving: 61 calories; 6 grams total fat; 3 mg sodium; 80 mg potassium; 2 grams carbohydrates; 0.8 grams fiber; 0 grams sugar; 2.3 grams protein

Spanish Rice

½ cup onions, chopped
1 tomato, chopped
½ cup red bell pepper, chopped
3 tablespoons olive oil
1 teaspoon chili powder
1 teaspoon sea salt
1 dash cayenne pepper
2 cups brown rice, uncooked
4 cups water

***

Sauté onion, tomato, bell pepper, salt, and cayenne pepper in olive oil until soft.
Add rice and toss for 3 minutes.
In medium saucepan, combine entire mixture. Pour in water and cover.
Bring to a boil, then lower heat. Simmer until rice is light and fluffy.
Yield: Serves 10

Nutrition Information:

Single serving: 69 calories; 4 grams total fat; 338 mg sodium; 99 mg potassium; 7 grams carbohydrates; 1 gram sugar; 0.9 grams protein

Desserts

Everyone waits anxiously for the dessert to cap off a good (or bad!) meal. These delicious recipes will add pizazz to your meals.

Banana Ice Cream

¾ cup raw cashews
¾ cup soymilk powder
3 cups pineapple juice
3 cups coconut milk
¾ cup orange juice concentrate
4 large bananas, ripe
3 cups crushed pineapple
1 teaspoon vanilla extract, non-alcohol
¼ teaspoon sea salt

***

Place cashews, soymilk powder, and pineapple juice in blender. Blend until smooth.
Add coconut milk and orange juice concentrate and blend again.
With blender still running, add bananas, crushed pineapple, vanilla, and salt.
Sweeten to taste
Place in freezer and serve frozen.
Yield: 1 gallon or 10 servings

Nutrition Information:

Single serving: 319 calories; 15 grams total fat; 19 mg sodium; 628 mg potassium; 46 grams carbohydrates; 3 grams fiber; 32 grams sugar; 5 grams protein

Blueberry Crisp

1 cup quick oats
½ cup unbleached flour
¾ cup turbinado sugar
½ cup Smart Balance margarine
4 cups blueberries (fresh or frozen)

2 tablespoons cornstarch
Sugar to sweeten berries
Cream Topping recipe (p. 96) or store-bought whipped cream or yogurt

***

Mix oats, flour, and sugar. Cut in margarine until mixture is crumbly.
Pack half of mixture into bottom of 8 x 8 pan.
In a small saucepan, bring berries, cornstarch, and sugar to boil until thick.
Cover oat mixture with berry filling, then top with remaining crumb mixture.
Cover pan or baking dish with freezer wrap, and freeze.
Bake, unthawed, at 350° for 1 hour.
Serve warm, cut into squares. Top with whipped cream, yogurt, or Cream Topping recipe.
Yield: Serves 8

Nutrition Information:

Single serving: 142 calories; 3 grams total fat; 85 mg sodium; 64.7 grams potassium; 28 grams carbohydrates; 19 grams sugar; 1 gram protein

Coconut Macaroons

1 ⅓ cup shredded coconut
⅓ cup turbinado sugar
⅛ teaspoon sea salt

2 tablespoons unbleached flour
2 egg whites, or equivalent egg substitute
½ teaspoon almond extract, non-alcohol

***

Preheat oven to 325 degrees.
Combine coconut, sugar, salt, and flour in bowl.
Stir in egg whites and almond flavoring. Mix well.
Drop mixture by the teaspoon onto greased baking sheet.
Bake for 20 minutes, until edges are browned. Remove immediately.
Yield: Serves 18

Nutrition Information:

Single serving: 79 calories; 1.5 grams total fat; 21 mg sodium; 20 grams carbohydrates; 18 grams sugar

Desserts

Easy Banana Pudding

1 (5-ounce) box vanilla pudding/pie filling
½ box firm silken tofu
1 box vanilla wafers, made with non-hydrogenated oils
6 large ripe bananas, sliced
Cream Topping recipe (p. 96), optional

***

Blend pudding mix and tofu until smooth.
In tall dish with sides, add a layer of wafers, bananas, and some pudding.
Repeat layers until all ingredients are used. End with vanilla wafers on top.
Refrigerate until ready to serve.
Yield: Serves 8

Nutrition Information:

Single serving: 382 calories; 11 grams total fat; 213 mg sodium; 493 mg potassium; 70 grams carbohydrates; 4 grams fiber; 16 grams sugar; 4 grams protein

Famous Sugarless Apple Pie

1 (6-ounce) can frozen apple juice, no sugar added, thawed
1 ½ tablespoons cornstarch
1 tablespoon cold water
Whole Wheat Pie Crust recipe (p. 94)
3 tablespoons Smart Balance® margarine
6 medium red delicious apples, peeled and sliced, about 6 cups

***

Preheat oven to 350 degrees.
Pour thawed apple juice into saucepan. Add cinnamon.
Smooth cornstarch in cold water and add to saucepan. Bring to boil.
Reduce heat and simmer until mixture thickens.
In a 10-inch pie pan with 2-inch deep sides, fill pastry shell/crust with apples.
Pour apple juice mixture over apples and dot with margarine on top.
Cover with top crust. Prick with fork in several places, allowing steam to escape.
Bake for 50 minutes, or until crust is golden brown and the filling is bubbly.
Yield: Serves 8

Nutrition Information:

Single serving: 24 calories; 2 grams total fat; 36 mg sodium; 982 mg potassium; 2 grams carbohydrates; 22 grams fiber; 0 grams sugar; 2.4 grams protein

Fruit Cocktail Delight

A light, refreshing dessert!

2 cans fruit cocktail in light syrup, drained
1 can pineapple chunks, drained
1 cup coconut, shredded
1 cup maraschino cherries, drained
1 cup walnuts, chopped
Cream Topping recipe (p. 96)

***

Mix all ingredients in bowl.
Fold in Cream Topping to desired consistency.
Yield: Serves 10

Nutrition Information:

Single serving: 161 calories; 4 grams total fat; 21 mg sodium; 209 mg potassium; 31 grams carbohydrates; 3 grams fiber; 26 grams sugar; 1 gram protein

Fruit Gelatin

4 cups fruit juice of choice
2 tablespoons agar powder (gelatin)
1 ½ cups canned fruit of choice, drained
½ cup walnuts, chopped

Cream Topping:
¼ cup cashews
1 cup water
½ cup coconut
1 cup soy milk
1 teaspoon vanilla, alcohol free

***

Heat juice and gelatin (agar powder) in saucepan until gelatin is dissolved.
Remove from heat. Add fruit and nuts, then pour into mold or bowl.
Chill.
For cream topping, toast cashews in oven. Blend cashews in water until creamy texture. Add remaining topping ingredients. Continue to blend for about 3 minutes.
Serve gelatin in individual parfait glasses with Cream Topping recipe.
Yield: Serves 8

Nutrition Information:

Single serving: 372 calories; 11 grams total fat; 64 mg sodium; 66 grams carbohydrates; 1 gram fiber; 61 grams sugar; 1 gram protein

Molasses Cookies

2 cups unbleached flour
1 cup molasses
1 cup quick oats
½ cup canola oil
½ cup pecans or walnuts, chopped
½ cup raisins
1 teaspoon sea salt
1 tablespoon vanilla extract, non-alcohol

***

Preheat oven to 325 degrees.
Place all ingredients in a bowl and mix.
Drop mixture by spoonful onto ungreased cookie sheet.
Bake for 15–20 minutes until light brown.
Yield: Serves 12

Nutrition Information:

Single serving: 282 calories; 15 grams total fat; 270 mg sodium; 224 mg potassium; 33 grams carbohydrates; 2 grams fiber; 6 grams sugar; 3 grams protein

Orange Sherbet

2 ripe bananas
1 (16-ounce) can crushed pineapple
½ cup undiluted orange juice concentrate

***

Combine all ingredients in blender and blend until smooth.
Pour into freezer trays and freeze until slightly frozen.
Remove from freezer and whip with beater. Return to freezer until firm.
Yield: Serves 4

Nutrition Information:

Single serving: 151 calories; 0 grams total fat; 2 mg sodium; 480 mg potassium; 39 grams carbohydrates; 3 grams fiber; 29 grams sugar; 1 gram protein

Pecan Pie

½ cup turbinado sugar
½ cup maple syrup
2 large eggs, or equivalent egg substitute
1 teaspoon vanilla extract, alcohol-free

2 tablespoon Smart Balance@ margarine
2 ½ cups pecans, chopped
1 pie crust, unbaked (If store bought, use one made with vegetable shortening.)

***

Cook sugar and syrup in medium saucepan until slightly thick. Remove from heat.
Beat eggs gently in separate bowl. Pour into hot syrup mixture while beating.
Add vanilla and nuts after eggs and syrup are mixed well.
Pour into crust.
Bake at 300° for 1 hour.
Serve with Cream Topping recipe (p. 96), whipped cream, or vanilla yogurt.
Yield: Serves 8

Nutrition Information:

Single serving: 309 calories; 24 grams total fat; 59 mg sodium; 157 mg potassium; 25 grams carbohydrates; 3 grams fiber; 13 grams sugar; 4 grams protein

Pumpkin Pie with Pecan Topping

1 can pumpkin puree
1 cup coconut milk
¾ cup turbinado sugar
1 tablespoon cornstarch
½ tablespoon nutmeg
½ teaspoon sea salt
½ teaspoon cinnamon or coriander
1 pie crust, unbaked
Pecan Crumble Topping recipe (p. 99)

***

Combine all ingredients in bowl.
Pour into unbaked pie crust.
Top with Pecan Crumble Topping recipe.
Bake at 350° for 1 hour.
Yield: Serves 8

Nutrition Information:

Single serving: 167 calories; 6 grams total fat; 33 mg sodium; 361 mg potassium; 31 grams carbohydrates; 12 grams fiber; 7 grams sugar; 3 grams protein

Strawberry Shortcake

2 cups unbleached flour
2 tablespoons turbinado sugar
1 tablespoon baking powder, aluminum-free
½ teaspoon sea salt
½ cup Smart Balance® margarine
1 egg, or equivalent egg substitute
1 cup soy milk
1 teaspoon vanilla extract, alcohol-free
Strawberry Filling recipe (p. 100)

***

In medium bowl, stir together flour, sugar, baking powder, and salt.

Cut in margarine until mixture turns into coarse crumbs.

In separate bowl, beat together egg, milk, and vanilla. Add to flour mixture, stirring with fork just enough to moisten.

Preheat oven to 450 degrees.

Spread dough into greased, 8-inch round baking pan.

Bake for 20 minutes, or until lightly browned.

Yield: Serves 8

Nutrition Information:

Single serving: 160 calories; 3 grams total fat; 474 mg sodium; 0 mg potassium; 30 grams carbohydrates; 7 grams sugar; 3 grams protein (Strawberry Filling nutrition information not included)

Sweet Potato Pie

4 cups cooked sweet potatoes, whipped
2 cups coconut milk
1 cup turbinado sugar
2 tablespoons Smart Balance® margarine
⅓ cup flour
1 tablespoon vanilla extract, alcohol-free
2 teaspoon Rumford® aluminum-free baking powder
1 teaspoon cinnamon or coriander
2 prepared crusts

***

Preheat oven to 350 degrees.
Combine all ingredients (except crusts) in a bowl and mix well.
Pour into unbaked crusts.
Bake for 50 minutes. It is done when you touch the center and it springs back, or when you pierce the center with a toothpick and it comes out clean.
Yield: Serves 8

Nutrition Information:

Single serving: 137 calories; 1 gram total fat; 192 mg sodium; 378 mg potassium; 31 grams carbohydrates; 27 grams sugar; 2 grams protein

Yellow Cake with Orange Glaze

⅔ cup Smart Balance® margarine
1 tablespoon vanilla extract, alcohol-free
1 cup turbinado sugar
1 tablespoon baking powder, aluminum-free
¾ teaspoon sea salt
2 ½ cups unbleached flour, sifted
1 cup soy milk
½ box firm silken tofu
2 tablespoons lemon juice
Orange Glaze recipe (p. 98)

***

Preheat oven to 350 degrees.
All ingredients must be at room temperature.
Mix margarine with vanilla just to soften.
Add sugar, baking powder, and salt to margarine mixture. Beat well.
Add flour, then milk, and beat 2 minutes at medium speed.
Add tofu and lemon juice and mix 1 minute more.
Spoon batter into greased and floured bunt pan, or 2 cake pans.
Bake for 30 minutes. Done when light brown and firm to the touch.
Let cool slightly. Turn pan upside down to place cake onto serving dish.
Apply Orange Glaze recipe.
Yield: Serves 10

Nutrition Information:

Single serving: 330 calories; 5 grams total fat; 520 mg sodium; 0 mg potassium; 72 grams carbohydrates; 0 grams fiber; 68 grams sugar; 0 grams protein

Breads and Pie Crusts

There's nothing like a good piece of bread to complement a meal, or a quality crust to hold together a delicious dessert!

Golden Cornbread

1 cup yellow cornmeal
1 cup unbleached flour
2 teaspoons turbinado sugar
2 teaspoons baking powder, aluminum-free
½ teaspoon sea salt

2 cups soy milk, plain flavor
2 tablespoons canola oil
¼ cup egg substitute
Olive oil spray

***

Preheat oven to 400 degrees.
Sift cornmeal, flour, sugar, baking powder, and salt in bowl and mix well.
Add milk, oil, and egg substitute. Mix well.
Spray sides and bottom of flat baking dish. Pour in mixture.
Bake for 45 minutes, until golden brown.
Yield: Serves 12

Nutrition Information:

Single serving: 99 calories; 3 grams total fat; 337 mg sodium; 17 grams carbohydrates; 1 gram fiber; 1 gram sugar; 2 grams protein

Holiday Rolls

2 teaspoons active dry yeast
1 ½ cups warm water
1 cup Smart Balance® margarine, melted and divided
3 ½ cups unbleached flour
½ cup turbinado sugar
2 eggs, or equivalent egg substitute
1 teaspoon sea salt

***

Preheat oven to 350 degrees.
Dissolve yeast in water, according to package directions.
Add ½ cup margarine to yeast, setting the rest aside. Mix in remaining ingredients.
Let rise for 1 ½ hours.
Roll out on floured board until 1 inch thick.
Cut into dumpling-like pieces, approximately 1 ½ squares or circles, or use biscuit cutter.
Dip in remaining margarine and place in cake pans or baking pan with dough touching.
Let rise 30 minutes in warm kitchen, or oven.
Bake for 25 minutes or until light brown.
Yield: Serves 12

Nutrition Information:

Single serving: 262 calories; 10 grams total fat; 298 mg sodium; 99 mg potassium; 39 grams carbohydrates; 6 grams fiber; 5 grams protein

Memorable Cornbread Dressing/Stuffing

1 large onion, chopped
1 ½ cups celery, chopped
1 red bell pepper, chopped
4 cloves garlic, minced
Olive oil
Golden Cornbread recipe, baked (p. 88)
1 cup vegetable broth
2 cups soy milk, plain
1 cup veggie sausage, ground (optional)

***

Preheat oven to 350 degrees.
Sauté onion, celery, bell pepper, garlic, and sausage (optional) in oil.
In large bowl, add cornbread, broth, milk, and sautéed vegetables. Mix well.
Transfer to greased baking pan and cover with aluminum foil.
Bake for 1 hour until firm and lightly brown.
Yield: Serves 12

Nutrition Information:

Single serving: 56 calories; 4 grams total fat; 32 mg sodium; 138 mg potassium; 5 grams carbohydrates; 1.3 grams fiber; 0.2 grams sugar; 2 grams protein

Pie Crust

2 cups unbleached flour
½ cup canola oil
⅔ cup soy milk
½ teaspoon sea salt

***

Mix all ingredients in bowl.
Knead slightly.
Roll out evenly between 2 sheets of plastic wrap until ready to use.
Yield: Makes a double crust for 10-inch pie, or enough for 2 single crusts.

Nutrition Information:
Single serving: 230 calories; 14 grams total fat; 148 mg sodium; 23 grams carbohydrates; 3 grams protein

Pizza Crust

1 ½ cups warm water
2 teaspoons active dry yeast
2 tablespoons honey
1 teaspoon sea salt
3 cups unbleached flour
1 tablespoon vital wheat gluten flour

***

Mix all ingredients in bowl, according to order.
Form into two balls and spread into two pizza pans. Let rise.
Add pizza sauce, topping with any other vegetables of choice.
Yield: Serves 10

Nutrition Information:
Single serving: 16 calories; 236 mg sodium; 4 grams carbohydrates; 3 grams sugar

Walnut Raisin Muffins

2 cups unbleached flour
2 teaspoons baking powder, aluminum-free
½ teaspoon sea salt
½ cup Smart Balance® margarine
1 cup soy milk
½ cup maple syrup
½ cup raisins
½ cup walnut pieces
1 ripe banana, mashed
Olive oil spray

***

Preheat oven to 425 degrees.
Combine flour, baking powder, and salt. Mix well.
Melt margarine and let cool.
Combine margarine, milk, maple syrup, raisins, walnuts, and banana. Mix well.
Add to dry ingredients and stir only to moisten.
Fill greased muffin pan.
Bake for 35 minutes, until lightly brown.
Yield: 12 muffins

Nutrition Information:

Single serving: 211 calories; 8 grams total fat; 152 mg sodium; 218 mg potassium; 31 grams carbohydrates; 3 grams fiber; 14 grams sugar; 5 grams protein

Whole Wheat Bread

1 cup warm water
1 ½ teaspoons yeast
1 tablespoon molasses
2 tablespoons gluten flour

1 tablespoon olive oil
1 teaspoon sea salt
2–3 cups whole wheat flour

***

Mix water, yeast, and molasses. Allow to bubble.
Add remaining ingredients, adding enough flour to knead without being sticky.
Knead for 10 minutes, or until dough comes back when you poke it.
Shape into loaf or desired shape. Allow to rise in warm place until doubled in size.
Bake at 350° for 35 minutes.
Yield: 1 loaf

Nutrition Information:

Per slice: 110 calories; 3 grams total fat; 170 mg sodium; 18 grams carbohydrates; 3 grams fiber; 11 grams protein

Whole Wheat Pie Crust

1 ½ cups unbleached flour
1 cup whole wheat flour
2 tablespoons wheat germ
¾ teaspoon sea salt
½ cup canola oil
½ cup boiling water

***

Stir together flour, wheat germ, and salt.
Add oil and water. Mix until dry ingredients are moist.
Form into a ball and divide in half.
Roll out between 2 sheets of plastic wrap.
Yield: Makes a double crust for deep, 10-inch pie, or enough for 2 single crusts

Nutrition Information:

Single serving: 245 calories; 14 grams total fat; 221 mg sodium; 28 grams carbohydrates; 4 grams fiber; 3.75 grams protein

Toppings and Fillings

These toppings give the dietary advantage of 3 grams of fat each. Enjoy!

Cream Topping

¼ cup cashews, raw toasted
1 cup water
½ cup coconut
2 dates
1 cup soy milk
1 teaspoon vanilla, alcohol-free

***

Toast cashews in oven or toaster oven.
Blend cashews with water until creamy texture.
Add remaining ingredients and continue to blend.
Serve over blueberry crisp or other such desserts.
Yield: 8 servings

Nutrition Information:

Single serving: 45 calories; 2 grams total fat; 38 mg sodium; 4 grams carbohydrates; 4 grams sugar; 2 grams protein

Lasagna Tofu-style Filling

2 boxes firm tofu
4 tablespoons lemon juice
2 tablespoons nutritional yeast flakes
3 teaspoons sweet basil
2 teaspoons garlic powder
1 teaspoon onion powder
1 teaspoon sea salt
1 teaspoon turbinado sugar

***

Drain tofu and mash thoroughly with potato masher.
Mix with remaining ingredients until consistency of cottage cheese.
Yield: 4 cups

Nutrition Information:

Single serving: 34 calories; 2 grams total fat; 295 mg sodium; 136 mg potassium; 1 gram fiber; 5 grams protein; 0.6 grams sugar

Orange Glaze

¼ cup orange juice concentrate
¼ cup soy milk
3 tablespoons Smart Balance® margarine
¼ cup turbinado sugar, powdered in blender

***

In small saucepan bring orange juice, milk, and margarine to boil.
Remove from heat and let cool.
Fold in powdered sugar with fork.
Pour over yellow or white cake.
Yield: 10 servings

Nutrition Information:

Single serving: 52 calories; 3 grams total fat; 36 mg sodium; 57 mg potassium; 0.2 grams fiber; 1 gram sugar; 1 gram protein

Pecan Crumble Topping

1 cup Pie Crust Recipe, crumbled (p. 91)
½ cup turbinado sugar
⅓ cup pecans, chopped

***

Mix ingredients well, until crumbly.
Use to top pumpkin filling.

Nutrition Information:

Single serving: 72 calories; 4 grams total fat; 27 mg sodium; 21 mg potassium; 9 grams carbohydrates; 0.4 grams fiber; 0.2 grams sugar; 0.7 grams protein

Strawberry Filling

Strawberry Shortcake recipe (p. 84)
1 cup Cream Topping recipe (p. 96), divided
4 cups sweetened strawberries, halved and divided
Smart Balance® margarine, softened

***

Using a sharp knife, gently split shortcake horizontally in two layers.
Lift off top carefully and place bottom layer on serving plate.
Spread top with softened margarine.
Spoon on half of strawberries and Cream Topping.
Place second half cake on top of filling.
Add remaining strawberries and Cream Topping over the top.
Slice and serve.
Yield: 8 servings

Nutrition Information:

Single serving: 54 calories; 3 grams total fat; 21 mg sodium; 800 mg potassium; 2 grams carbohydrates; 1 gram fiber; 1 gram protein (Does not included shortcake information)

My Seven Favorite Menus

Planning a Meal

Menu One

>Spaghetti and Pecan Meatballs
>Best Tossed Salad
>Lip-smacking French Dressing
>Peas with Sliced Almonds
>Golden Cornbread

Menu Two

>Wok Vegetable Stir Fry with Tofu
>Tomato and Cucumber Salad
>Brown Rice
>Ginger Sauce
>Walnut and Raisin Muffins

Menu Three

>Baked Tofu
>Macaroni and Tofu Cheese
>Crunchy Cabbage
>Rolls

Menu Four

- Pinto Beans
- Brown Rice
- Carrot and Apple Salad
- Honey Beets
- Rolls

Menu Five

- Sausage and Noodle Casserole
- Fried Corn
- Best Tossed Salad
- Celery Dressing
- Bread

Menu Six

- Haystacks
- Fruit Cocktail Delight
- Molasses Cookies

Menu Seven

- Vegeburger Loaf
- Tofu Cheese and Potato Supreme
- Vegetable Platter (with marinade)
- Baby Lima Beans and Peas
- Rolls
- Yellow Cake with Orange Glaze

Additional Tips for Maintaining Good Health

Physical activity is essential to preserve the body's functions. Every part of the body performs better when we exercise. When we work out, we increase endurance, reduce stress, build energy, slow the aging process, build muscle density, strengthen bones, increase flexibility, decrease body fat, and keep heart and blood vessels healthy.

For diabetics, experts found that a 15 to 30-minute walk after each meal helps burn extra sugar in the blood.[1] (Diehl and Ludington, 2012) Others should exercise from 30 to 60 minutes per day. Any movement activity counts!

Take the children outside or go to the park. Let them run and play, or simply take a walk. Lawn work or gardening can be perfect ways to stay healthy.

It's your choice. However, check with your health care professional before starting a vigorous workout program.

Every living thing needs **water** to stay alive. Most of us don't drink enough clean, clear water. Even going two or three days without it can be extremely harmful. Our bodies contain more water than anything else (women 60

---

[1] Hans Diehl and Aileen Ludington, *Health Power: Healthy By Choice, Not by Chance* (Hagerstown, MD: Review and Herald Publishing, 2012), p. 55.

percent, men 70 percent), and we need to maintain that balance. Just a 20 percent loss of the body's water can cause death.

Let's look at the role water plays in our system: It transports nutrients, oxygen, hormones, disease-fighting cells, and waste matter to and from body organs via the blood stream and lymphatic vessels. Water lubricates joints, muscles, ligaments, skin, and mucous membranes. Water acts as the body's air conditioner by regulating body temperature, and it aids digestion and breathing. It can be a tonic, stimulant, and sedative.

Nutritionists suggest we drink an average of six to eight (8-ounce) glasses a day, although changes in weather or the amount of activity performed may require more. It is best to take a planned approach to drinking water. For instance, upon rising in the morning, drink two glasses, then another two glasses mid-morning, then two more glasses mid-afternoon. Finish the evening with two more before six pm.

A word of caution, however: It is best to drink water, or any beverage, 15 to 30 minutes before eating, or 1 to 2 hours after meals. This practice improves digestion, as all liquid is absorbed before any food is digested. When drinking with a meal, food stays in the stomach longer than it should—sometimes days—which impedes digestion, resulting in indigestion, acid reflux, and other stomach issues.

Every living organism cannot exist without the presence of natural **sunshine**. It provides energy for plant growth, in turn providing food for humans and animals, and warmth for Earth and its inhabitants. It causes the formation of vitamin D and kills viruses, bacteria, molds, and germs in the air. It decreases stress, builds the immune system, reduces insomnia, lifts the mood, gives skin a healthy glow, and thickens the skin, giving you more resistance to injury and infection. It also reduces blood pressure and cholesterol levels and can treat sinusitis and arthritis.

Experts have determined that getting as much as 15 to 20 minutes of sun exposure a day will keep us healthy. Darker skin, however, needs a little more.

Pure Air—There is so much confusion today about the environment and the pollutants that are spewed into our atmosphere, making it difficult to make educated choices. Some scientists declare that we have nothing to be concerned about, while others caution that we're in trouble.

So, what are we to do? We can control our small space with some planning. Just as there are pollutants in the outside atmosphere, a large number also accumulate within the inside environment of our homes. Indoor pollution includes tobacco smoke, radon (enters homes from the ground in some regions), chemicals released from synthetic carpets and furniture, pesticides, household cleansers, and poor ventilation.

We can reduce indoor levels by continually circulating fresh air. Open the windows at a safe position, especially during the morning hours, when there are less pollutants outside. This fresh air can improve blood pressure and lower the heart rate, and it creates a cleansing action in the lungs. It also helps hay fever and other respiratory symptoms.

Plants and animals grow faster with pure air. Add green plants to every room in the home to keep air fresh. Good air also enables better relaxation. A perfect way to relax is to go outside when the air is fresh and breathe deeply, 10 to 15 times, slowly from the abdomen, after each meal and just before going to bed.

Balance is one word we all can talk about. Most of us have already determined we need more balance or self-control in some aspects of our lives. It's a good idea to abstain from everything which is harmful to us and use good judgment in that which is helpful to our health.

This is hard to achieve without truly making some lifestyle changes. All the aforementioned health tips focus on balancing your life. Dr. Selye (Diehl and Ludington, 2012) a specialist in diseases that affect the glands, makes this observation:

I have never seen a person who died of old age. In fact, I do not think anyone has ever died of old age yet. To die of old age would mean that all the organs of the body had worn out proportionally, merely by having been used too long. This is never the case. We invariably die because one vital part has worn out too early in proportion to the rest of the body.

There is always one part that wears out first and wrecks the whole human machinery merely because the other parts cannot function without it.

The lesson seems to be that as far as man can regulate his life by voluntary actions, he should seek to equalize stress throughout his being. The human body—like the tires on a car or the rug on a floor—wears longest when it wears evenly.[2]

---

2   Hans Diehl and Aileen Ludington, *Health Power: Healthy By Choice, Not by Chance* (Hagerstown, MD: Review and Herald Publishing, 2012), p. 200.

Rest is necessary in the fast-paced, demanding, and exhausting life of today. We never seem to have enough hours in a day to accomplish all we aspire to do. Some seventy million people have too little or very disturbed sleep every night. Studies show that we need different kinds of rest, and a good night's sleep is unavoidably important.

Newborn babies sleep from 16 to 20 hours per day. Young children need 10 to 12 hours, teenagers need an average of 9 hours, and adults do best on 7 to 8 hours per night. We can likely see that most of us are lacking in this area, and we are paying the price in more cases of depression than ever, along with the rise in illnesses and automobile accidents.

We need to slow down and take several breaks during the workday. While daily watching the little squirrels from my kitchen window as they run up and down the trees, gathering nuts, and strengthening their nests with leaves and twigs, I think they must have an inborn clock that tells them when to take a break. By instinct they all go up to their nests at the same time, several times a day. It is fascinating to see them conduct their schedules so regularly.

Humans seems to be just the opposite; we don't know when to stop and rest. But here's how a good night's sleep affects us: The deep rest allows the body to renew itself. Rest aids in healing of injuries, infections, stress, and emotional traumas. Rest strengthens the immune system and protects us from disease. It can add length to our lives.

Maintain as regular a schedule as possible for going to bed. Studies show that when we go to bed before ten p.m. and sleep through to two a.m., our bodies heal themselves and we receive twice the amount of rest in those hours. We also sleep better in a completely dark room because it builds up our melatonin levels. If you can, crack the bedroom window just a tad so the fresh air can enhance better sleep. You will have more energy in the morning.

Having a regular time for eating and exercising also aids the body, since the body flourishes on regular rhythms. Eat the evening meal at least four hours before bedtime, because an empty stomach is best for good rest.

Remember, caffeine in coffee, tea, or cola is a stimulant to the central nervous system and will result in insomnia. Alcoholic beverages have the same effect on our sleep.

Trust in divine power drastically affects our wellbeing. We humans are more than physical, mental, and emotional beings—we're also spiritual beings. If the other areas of our lives are maintained and the spiritual side neglected, we do not have total health and wellbeing. There is no separation of these components in life. Believing in a power larger than ourselves is paramount, for we are fragile and will soon learn that we're powerless against many circumstances. We can easily lose hope in the face of problems we can't readily solve.

Research has proven that when we harbor such things as anger, fear, resentment, and distrust, it can produce effects on the body that weaken the immune system and eventually lead to disease. But when positive emotions like love, joy, faith, and trust strengthen the immune system, they protect the body from disease.

Health and fitness are not enough. Neither is power, wealth, prestige, or beauty. At the root of our being is the need for greater purpose in life. This need can only be filled from a knowledge and relationship with the higher power we call God, who alone can bring balance and peace of mind, resulting in wellbeing.

Why not enjoy a life of abundant living? You and your family deserve it, and at the same time you can reduce your food costs, doctor visits, weight gain, and energy loss.

If you're experiencing a lifestyle disease, following these guidelines may provide another added benefit. By implementing these health principles, disease can reverse itself. Moreover, these tips and recipes work to balance the body to prevent lifestyle diseases from occurring in the first place. Take the move from a humdrum life to a new life of adventure!

Success Stories

These are real cases the author and her husband consulted on while conducting health seminars.

Hypertension and Obesity

Sharon is in her early fifties. She has suffered from high blood pressure and obesity most of her adult life and was on many medications. Upon attending a health seminar in her town, she got personal counseling and implemented the full eight-step program outlined in this cookbook. After six months, her doctor took her off all previous medications and she lost fifty pounds. Incidentally, the hypertension is gone, too.

Sharon is a new woman now, with lots of energy. Friends and family are asking how she did it without going on a diet.

Diabetes and Obesity

Pastor J. was taking many units of insulin to control his diabetes, and his obesity added to the problem. He was on medications for both, yet he wasn't seeing any improvements. Eventually he attended a health seminar and personal counseling session. He started immediately on the eight-step program.

One day, due to bad weather, my husband and I were getting in our walking exercise at the mall when we heard someone calling our name behind us. We stopped and turned around as the gentleman ran up to us and said, "You don't remember me, do you?"

We couldn't place him at first, but then he informed us of the health consultation and shared his results. He looked ten years younger! He lost weight and was able to come off the insulin and high blood pressure meds. What a transformation!

Coronary Heart Disease

For Pastor B, it was becoming unbearable for him to walk even a short distance without experiencing shortness of breath, and he couldn't carry his own briefcase. He had gone through an operation but experienced no change. His health was declining rapidly.

His doctor had given him six months to live, and he began to place his affairs in order. Then he heard of a seminar at his church and opted for a consultation. His wife started him on the program right away. He couldn't walk, but he put the other parts of the program immediately into practice.

After three months, his doctor noticed he was walking better and decided to give him some tests. Pastor B's health was improving! The doctor advised him to keep up whatever he was doing, and within six months the Pastor was doing fine—and test results proved it!

***

You might be asking how one program can reverse three different maladies? Well, all three diseases were caused by lifestyle. When the lifestyle changed, the disease reversed itself—because our bodies are designed to heal themselves if placed in the right environment.

You too can receive a favorable outcome, whether you are experiencing a lifestyle disease or simply wanting to avoid an illness. Take account of your lifestyle choices, apply these healthy principles, and enjoy a greater degree of wellbeing!

Stock Your Pantry

A Glossary of Healthy Ingredients

Agar powder:
A gelatin product, made from seaweed, to thicken foods.

Alcohol-free extracts:
Flavor extracts that contain no alcohol while still maintaining flavor strength. Regular extracts contain thirty-five percent or more alcohol.

Aluminum-free baking powder:
Many brands of baking powder contain non-anodized aluminum. Rumford® is a brand that contains no aluminum residue.

Bragg® All-purpose Seasoning:
An unfermented soy sauce made from organic soybeans and distilled water. It is lower in sodium than other soy sauces, which are fermented and may lead to stomach problems.

Cardamom:
A natural condiment, non-irritating to the stomach, often used instead of nutmeg. You'll want to buy it ground and you can find it in the spice aisle.

Chicken or Beef-style Seasoning:
A mixture of herbs and seasonings added to give foods a meat-like flavor. One commercial brand is McKay's®.

Choplets®:
Canned textured vegetable protein (TVP) formed into chops and sliced.

Coriander:
A natural condiment, non-irritating to the stomach, often used instead of cinnamon. You'll want to buy it ground and you can find it in the spice aisle.

Egg substitutes:
Many substitutes are available in liquid form, such as Egg Beaters® (whites of egg, contains no cholesterol). You can find them in powdered form and just add water.

Flaxseeds:
Grind these seeds to use in place of eggs in recipes: 1 tablespoon flaxseed with 3 tablespoons water equals 1 egg, as used in bread and cookie recipes.

Gravy Master Seasoning and Browning Sauce®:
A liquid soy protein used to darken gravy. It adds texture and color to foods.

Liquid Smoke:
A substance produced from smoke passed through water, used for both food preservation and flavoring.

Morningstar Farms® products:
A brand of soy-based meat analogs found in major supermarkets. These products typically come in patties, links, or ground form.

Nutritional yeast flakes:
These flakes are usually yellow with cheese-like flavor and are good in gravies and sauces. Check your local health food store.

Sea Salt:
Evaporated seawater that is dried and ground into table salt consistency, unlike regular table salt that is chemically processed.

Tofu:
Fresh soybean curd: A good source of protein that comes in silken or fresh water packed, and in soft, medium, firm, or extra firm textures. Organic soybeans recommended.

Tofu Cheddar Cheese:
Yellow soybean product that is flavored and textured like cheese.

Turbinado Sugar:
A crystal liquid that remains from raw cane sugar, with a touch of molasses for coloring.

Unbleached Flour:
All-purpose flour that maintains its outer coating, which houses the nutrients.

Veggie Burger:
Textured, soy-based protein ground into burgers to replace ground beef in recipes.

Bibliography

1. Buettner, Dan. *"The Secrets of Living Longer." National Geographic*, Publication No. 5, 5th ed. Vol. 208, 2005.

2. CASAColumbia. "The Importance of Family Dinners 2012." Partnership to End Addiction. Partnership to End Addiction, September 2012. https://drugfree.org/reports/the-importance-of-family-dinners-viii.

3. Diehl, Hans, and Aileen Ludington. Health Power: Healthy By Choice, Not by Chance. Hagerstown, MD: Review and Herald Publishing Association, 2012.

4. McGrady, Darren. *Eating Royally: Recipes and Remembrances from a Palace Kitchen*. Nashville, TN: T. Nelson, 2007.

5. USDA. "Dietary Guidelines for Americans 2015-2020." ChooseMyPlate. Accessed Month Day, Year. https://www.choosemyplate.gov/eathealthy/dietary-guidelines.

6. White, Ellen G. *The Adventist Home.* Hagerstown, MD: Review and Herald Publishing Association, 1952.

About the Author

When Etta R. Montague Collins began to study and work toward experiencing better health for herself and her family, she wanted to make every aspect delicious and exciting, such as the transition to a plant-based diet. With each new recipe, her gauge on its success was based on whether her children responded favorably. They'd say, "Mom, this tastes good." She'd reply, "I prepared it with love."

She still feels that way. Much wisdom and enthusiasm has gone into each recipe creation. They've been tested over and over to make sure anyone can achieve excellent results. It is her passion to help others live their best life possible.

Consequently, she and her husband, Ed, travel throughout the United States conducting health seminars and cooking schools. She holds a Bachelor of Arts degree in print journalism from Metropolitan State University in Denver, Colorado.

Alphabetical Recipe Index

B

Baby Lima Beans and Peas 30, 102
Baked French Fries 62
Baked Macaroni and Cheese 12
Baked Tofu 13, 101
Banana and Sweet Potato Soufflé 31
Banana Ice Cream 74
Barbecue Tofu 13
Best Tossed Salad 42, 101, 102
Black-eyed Peas and Okra 32
Blueberry Crisp 75
Broccoli Rice 63

C

Cabbage Rolls 14
Carrot and Apple Salad 43, 102
Celery Dressing 50, 102
Choplets® Loaf 15
Coconut Macaroons 76
Cool Banana and Cherry Drink 63
Cream Topping 75, 77, 78, 79, 82, 96, 100
Crunchy Cabbage and Red Bell Pepper 33
Cucumber Dressing 50

D

Delectable Vegetable Stew 16

E

Easy Banana Pudding 77
Easy Brown Gravy 56
Easy Vegetable Soup 64
Excellent Sandwich Spread 65

F

Famous Sugarless Apple Pie 78
Flaky Brown Rice 21, 28, 66
Fried Corn 33, 102
Fruit Cocktail Delight 78, 102
Fruit Drink 67
Fruit Gelatin 79
Fruit Pizza 68

G

Garlic Spinach 34
Ginger Sauce 28, 56, 101
Golden Cornbread 88, 90, 101

H

Haystacks Combo 17
Hearty Trail Mix 69
Holiday Rolls 89
Honey Beets 35, 102
Honey Sesame Dressing 45, 51

L

Lasagna 18, 97
Lasagna Tofu-style Filling 97
Layered Salad 44
Lip-smacking French Dressing 51, 101
Low-cal Chili 19

M

Macaroni Salad 44
Make It Your Way Pizza 59, 70
Marinade for Vegetable Platter 40, 52

Alphabetical Recipe Index

Memorable Cornbread Dressing 90
Mixed Fruit Salad 45
Mixed Greens 36
Molasses Cookies 80, 102
Mom's Brown Gravy 57

N

Nutty Yellow Cheese Sauce 58

O

Orange Glaze 86, 98, 102
Orange Sherbet 81

P

Peas with Sliced Almonds 38, 101
Pecan Crumble Topping 83, 99
Pecan Meatballs 20, 24, 101
Pecan Pie 82
Pinto Beans and Brown Rice 21
Pizza Crust 91
Pizza Sauce 59, 70
Potato Salad 46

R

Rolled Oat Patties 22
Rolled Oat Patty Broth 60

S

Sausage and Noodle Casserole 23, 102
Savory Cauliflower and Zucchini 38
Scrambled Tofu 71
Spaghetti and Pecan Meatballs 24, 101
Spanish Rice 72
Strawberry Filling 84, 100
Strawberry Shortcake 84, 100
Sweet Potato Pie 85

T

Taco Salad 46
Tofu Cheese and Potato Supreme 25, 102
Tomato and Cucumber Salad 47, 101
Twice Baked Sweet Potatoes 39

V

Vegeburger Loaf 27, 102
Vege-links and Baked Beans 26
Vegetable and Spaghetti Salad Dressing 48, 53
Vegetable Platter 40, 52, 102

W

Walnut Raisin Muffins 92

Y

Yellow Cake with Orange Glaze 86, 102

TEACH Services, Inc.
P U B L I S H I N G

We invite you to view the complete
selection of titles we publish at:
www.TEACHServices.com

We encourage you to write us
with your thoughts about this,
or any other book we publish at:
info@TEACHServices.com

TEACH Services' titles may be purchased in
bulk quantities for educational, fund-raising,
business, or promotional use.
bulksales@TEACHServices.com

Finally, if you are interested in seeing
your own book in print, please contact us at:
publishing@TEACHServices.com

We are happy to review your manuscript at no charge.

www.ingramcontent.com/pod-product-compliance
Lightning Source LLC
Chambersburg PA
CBHW041244240426
43670CB00027B/2987